TO THE
TAIL

TALK

TO THE
TAIL

Jeanne Willis

Illustrated by
Isabella Grott

Collins

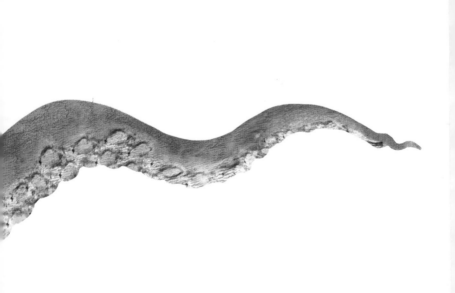

Contents

1 What the dog said

My name is Charlie, and this is my dog, Scruffy. He's been my loyal companion for years and he's the cleverest dog in the entire world.

It's true.
I'm a genius!

Obviously, Scruffy can understand simple words like sit, stay and fetch.

I understand dinner!
Hope it's sausages.

3

But the most amazing thing about Scruffy is that, somehow, he can work out whether I'm happy, miserable or even if I'm ill. Honestly, I have no idea how he manages it.

Doggy superpowers! I can read you with my nose and ears.

Scruffy Rhyme

I read you with my nose and ears,
I smell your fear, I hear your tears
I don't need words. I bark and growl
And if I'm lonely, hear me HOWL!

5

Amazing dog facts

Dogs are over 40 times better at detecting smells than humans. Some dogs can even smell medical conditions in people!

Dogs' ears are much more sensitive than human ears. They can hear higher pitched sounds that we cannot hear. They can hear four times the distance people can!

Dogs can see further than humans and can see much better than us in the dark too. However, they don't see colour the same way that people do.

7

Scruffy has his own special dog language.
His barks, howls and growls all have their
own **unique** and different meaning. He also
uses his body language to express himself.

Sometimes I have absolutely no idea
what he's going on about, but hey,
I'm only human.

Let me make this easy
for you. Why don't you
take a look at my Dog
Dictionary?

Scruffy's Dog Dictionary

Sound and posture	Meaning
Medium bark, relaxed posture, tail wag	Hello, my friend!
Short barks, bottom up, wagging tail	Play with me.
Whimpering and whining, tail tucked, trembling	I'm scared.
Grunting, rolled on back with tummy up	I feel safe with you.
Snarling, growling, teeth exposed, ears back	I'm angry!

I decided to listen, watch and try to learn what Scruffy is saying in dog language.

Maybe I could even find out how other species communicate. It would be cool to talk like a tiger, or even an elephant! So Scruffy and I went on a trip to the Safari Park to find out more.

On the way, Scruffy met his good friend, Cyril the sausage dog.

I don't know why they always sniff each other's bottoms. It's rude!

It's not rude if you're a dog. Our unique bottom smells reveal so much about us.

You've been eating chicken, right?

Talk to the tail

Here are some dog tail positions and what they can mean.

down - submissive

up - excited/ alert

broad strokes - happy

short strokes - worried

12

See how many you can spot when you're next out.

wagging left
– concerned

wagging right
– confident

wagging fast
– very excited

moving slowly
– less enthusiastic

Talk to the head

blinking
– friendly

eyebrow raising
– alert

head tilting
– curious

lip licking
– worried

squinting

– content

ear flattening

– scared

side eye

– nervous

nose wrinkling

– angry

2 What the tiger said

Safari Park

Assistance Dogs
are allowed
free entry!

I take Scruffy with me everywhere.
I have **epilepsy** and he can detect if
I'm about to have a fit.

He warns me so I can
get help in time.

You smell
good to go!

I heard a tiger roaring in the distance, so
we walked towards it to investigate.

Amazing tiger facts

Tigers are the largest wild cats in the world.

They are carnivores and only eat meat.

Tigers can sprint at over 60 kilometres an hour!

Tigers can live to be 25 years old.

Tigers are solitary and usually hunt alone at night.

A group of tigers is called an 'ambush' or a 'streak'.

Tigers have stripy skin as well as stripy fur.

A tiger's roar can be heard from three kilometres away.

There's the tiger, Scruffy!

I made some observations to see if I could read the tiger's body language.

It scratched a tree and rubbed its cheek on the bark. Then it squirted the tree with wee!

See? I'm not the only one!

18

Tiger Rhyme

I scratch the tree, I rub my cheek,
It's just the way that tigers speak.
Why do I wet the trunk with wee?
The smell tells others it was me
And warns them all to keep away,
I'm in a *stinking* mood today!

19

A female tiger came slinking through the long grass. It greeted the male with a soft, chuffing noise. I guess it meant "hello" in tiger language.

They're chilling out. Note the relaxed tails.

We hadn't been watching long, when
three cubs appeared! They greeted their
mother by rubbing against her cheek,
bobbing their heads and making
a high-pitched whining sound.
But the peaceful scene didn't last long.

To my horror, the cubs began to fight.
The big one smacked the little one with
its paw and pinned it down in the grass.
Why wasn't the mother tiger trying to
save it?

Don't panic. They're just
play-fighting like puppies.

22

Just then, I heard an ominous roar
in the distance.

I heard it first – read
my tail. I'm scared!

The father tiger leapt to his feet, flattened
his ears and swished his tail.

Eek! Tail-swishing from
a tiger is never good.

23

Another tiger arrived. It stared at the father tiger, showed its teeth and snarled. I thought there was going to be a fight.

I can't look!

Thankfully, the father tiger chased the other male away.

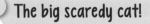

The big scaredy cat!

Here's how to talk like a tiger.

Scruffy's Tiger Dictionary

Sound and posture	Meaning
Head bobbing with whine	Hi Mum!
Relaxed tail, chuffing	Let's hang out together.
Scent-marking, scratching trees	This is my territory.
Snarling, swishing tail	Back off, I'm warning you!
Loud roar, flat ears, bared teeth	I may have to kill you.

3 What the bee said

Insect House

It was a hot day. After we'd seen the tigers,
I took Scruffy to the water bowls near
the Insect House.
I could tell he was thirsty
because his tongue was
hanging out and he
was panting.

I'm gasping!

We were about to go to the Aquarium
when I heard a loud humming sound.
There was a beehive in the wildflower
border by the Insect House. There were
bees everywhere, gathering **pollen** from
the foxglove flowers. Scruffy cocked his ear
and listened.

There was an audio button with information
about bees.

Amazing honey bee facts

A bee can produce about a tablespoon of honey in its lifetime.

A queen bee can lay up to 800,000 eggs in her lifetime.

Bees have two stomachs – one stomach for eating and another for storing nectar.

Honey was found in ancient pyramids in Egypt and it was still okay to eat!

Bees visit two million flowers to make one jar of honey.

Bees can fly up to 24 kilometres per hour.

Bees are the only insects in the world that make food that humans can eat.

Suddenly, Scruffy and I noticed a bee behaving oddly. The bee was doing a strange little dance.

It danced faster, waggling its **abdomen** and moving in the shape of an eight. It did a waggle run, turned to the right and went round in a circle. Then it turned left and repeated the steps.

I like the way it waggles! Wiggle-waggle, wiggle-waggle!

I couldn't help wondering why it was dancing.

Maybe it gives it a buzz!

Just then, the beekeeper arrived.

"Ah, you are witnessing the famous waggle dance," she said. "It's a form of bee communication."

The beekeeper explained that when a bee finds a new flower patch, the length of its dance tells other bees how far away the flowers are.

One of the bees did a different dance.
Instead of waggling, it shook itself.

The beekeeper told me bees do a "shake
dance" to show how much pollen is left in
the flowers. If there's plenty, they dance to
invite more bees to come to collect it.

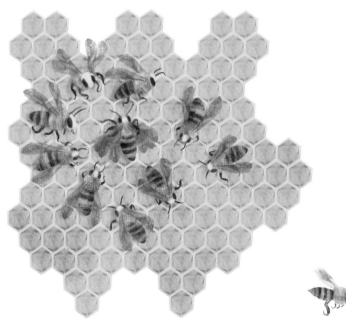

Bees communicate in other ways too, apparently. They even use smells to talk to each other! They produce different scents to say things like, "Look out, danger!" or "I'm going to sting you!" or "I'm the queen!"

Bees also use touch to work out whether other bees are friends or strangers.

Scruffy's Bee Rhyme

Touch feelers, touch feet
Are you friends, shall we meet?
Buzz off stranger, leave our hive
You shan't take our queen alive!

It's been fascinating learning how to talk like a bee.

Scruffy's Bee Dictionary

Sound and posture	Meaning
Buzz, buzz, waggle	I've found a great flower over there.
Buzz, buzz, touching feelers	Friend?
Buzz, buzz, shake, shake	There's lots of pollen and nectar left.
Whoop! (inaudible to human ear)	I'm so surprised!

Bees and their habitats

There are over 270 different kinds of bees in the UK. Here's where some of them might live.

Bumblebee
underground nest

Mason bee
hole in brickwork

Honey bee
hive

Mining bee
underground with
little volcano-shaped
pile of soil above

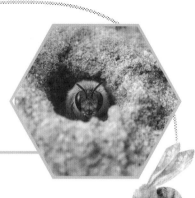

Leafcutter bee
hollow plant stem

Carpenter bee
hole in roof eaves

Sweat bee
hole in rotten wood

4 What the octopus said

I wanted to go straight to the Aquarium but Scruffy decided it was lunch time. I got a drink and a hot dog and gave him some of my sausage.

After lunch, we went to the Aquarium.
The woman at the desk gave me
a guidebook with blank pages at the back
which was handy for sketching things.

We saw **freshwater** fish, **tropical** fish and **marine** fish, including a tiger shark.

There were lots of other animals too. We spotted tanks full of sea urchins, lobsters and jellyfish but most of all, I wanted to talk to the octopus!

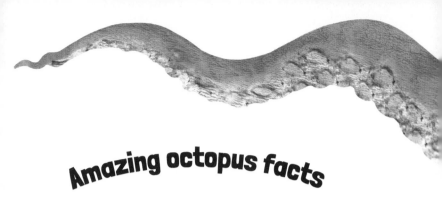

Amazing octopus facts

Octopuses have nine brains – one in their head and one in each arm. This means that each of their arms can taste, touch and do things on their own!

Octopuses can grow to 5.4 metres and move at speeds of 40 kilometres an hour.

They can squirt out ink to confuse predators.

They have three hearts.

Octopuses are highly intelligent and use tools. Some collect coconut shells to use as a mobile home.

The octopus watched me silently, clinging to the glass by its suckers. It had at least 240 suckers on each arm. Maybe it communicated by waving them.

What have you got to say for yourself, octopus?

I made a sketch of the octopus. It had
a beak but it couldn't sing like a bird.
It had big eyes with strange, rectangular
pupils, but it couldn't communicate by
blinking — it had no eyelids. Its skin was
pale and covered in tiny bumps but when
I looked again ...

... the octopus had changed colour!
While I was watching, it turned red and
started flashing. What did it mean? I tried
an experiment. I walked to the end of the
tank and it followed me! I put my hand
against the glass, and it reached out to
touch it.

It wants to
be my friend.

Well, it can't!
I'm your best friend.

I wondered if the octopus could turn other
colours, depending on its mood.

I didn't have to wonder for long. Just then,
another octopus appeared. I hadn't noticed
it before because it was the same colour as
the sand.

43

When the red octopus saw the sandy one, it turned jet black!

It swam to a pile of rocks and stood on two arms to make itself look taller.

Then it waved its arms furiously.

Uh-oh! It's in a dark mood.

The other octopus was so scared, it squirted ink and swam off!

Octopus Rhyme

Octopuses, strange as it might be
Can change their colour sleeping in the sea,
Some say that it seems
They're reacting to their dreams,
But what they dream of, no one can agree!

Scruffy's Octopus Dictionary

Sound and posture	Meaning
Silent, still and pale	I'm sleepy or relaxed.
Silent, flashing red	I'm friendly and playful.
Silent, dark, walking tall	Go away!
Silent, squirting black ink	I'm scared, I'm off!

Talk to the light

Some animals have organs that glow, flash
or make their body light up in the dark.

krill

jellyfish

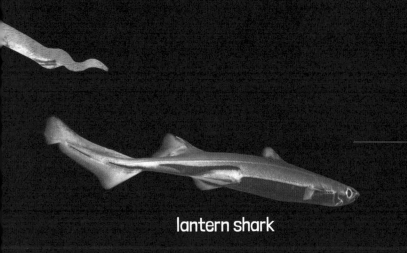

lantern shark

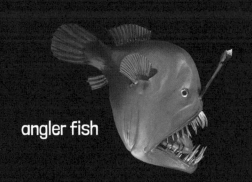

angler fish

This light is used to attract mates, scare predators and to communicate.

5 What the elephant said

After the Aquarium, we walked towards the Elephants' Habitat.

Amazing elephant facts

Elephants have the largest brains of any land animal.

They never forget and they can even remember other elephants and humans they met years before.

Elephants are the largest land animals in the world.

They can live for up to 70 years.

Baby elephants suck their trunks for comfort.

I wanted to find out how elephants communicate with each other.

There was a sound machine by the elephant paddock. I pressed it to hear and experience all the different sounds that elephants can make. They can rumble, snort, bark, roar, chirp and trumpet.

Trumpet? Can they play the violin too?

We saw a family of elephants – a mother and two young elephants. The mother elephant came over to see us. She had tiny eyes but huge ears. Apparently, elephants have poor eyesight but excellent hearing. They can hear another elephant trumpeting eight kilometres away.

They can hear better than me?!

Elephants also make very low-pitched sounds called infra-sounds that humans can't hear. They use these sounds to send secret messages to their relatives.

I was amazed at the size of the mother elephant's feet. They were over 40 centimetres wide. Did you know that elephants can "hear" by picking up vibrations they receive through their feet?

That's nothing! I can pick up mud in my feet.

I watched a baby elephant playing with
a tyre. He was playing happily until his big
sister came along to sabotage his fun and
stole the tyre. The baby elephant spread his
ears and stood tall – elephant sign language
for "I'm angry!"

The mother elephant stroked the baby with her trunk to soothe him. Family means everything to elephants. When they meet a long-lost relative, they link trunks and perform a greeting **ceremony**.

Elephant Rhyme

Elephants are clever!
They remember you forever.
Please be very careful what you say,
They use their trunks and ears
To share their hopes and fears
And tusks, if you are rude in any way.

The elephants walked off and sheltered under a tree. Apparently, they are able to tell if a storm is coming. Five minutes later, the sky went dark and I heard thunder above.

It began to rain, so we ran indoors.

Scruffy's Elephant Dictionary

Sound and posture	Meaning
Silent, ears lifted, trunk to ground	I hear my sister has found water.
Loud trumpet, ears spread, tusks lifted	I'm angry.
Chirps, flapping ears, linked trunks	I missed you!
Trumpeting, stiff tail, head low	I'm scared!

6 What the gorilla said

After a snack at the cafeteria, we had time to visit one more animal. I wanted to learn how gorillas communicate. We sailed to Gorilla Island and the guide gave us some great information.

Amazing gorilla facts

Gorillas are primates and live in family groups called a troop.

At night, gorillas sleep in nests made of leaves and branches.

A male gorilla called a silverback is chosen to lead the troop.

After chimpanzees and bonobos, gorillas are our closest relatives.

Gorilla Island was planted like a forest
with ropes to swing on and a tree house.
Gorillas are gentle but powerful.
A silverback can be as strong as
20 humans, so we watched from
the boat to make sure that we didn't
disturb them, and no one got hurt.

58

The gorilla family on the island had
eight members. There were five females,
two babies and a huge silverback.
The babies behaved like me and my sister!
They teased each other, played chase
and screamed.

And they burped!

The guide explained that gorillas communicate in a **variety** of ways. Although they can't speak, they can make over 22 different sounds from playful chuckles to frightened screams. The females we saw on the island were chuckling together like old friends sharing a joke.

The gorillas used lots of facial expressions similar to ours. If the babies annoyed the silverback, he gave them a stern stare with his lips pressed tightly together. He reminded me of someone – who was it? My dad in a bad mood!

I wouldn't pick a fight with him!

The gorillas were also big on body language and used lots of **gestures**, just like humans. I saw them wave, beckon, clap, drum and thump. At one point, the silverback beat his chest to remind everyone he was in charge.

Gorilla Rhyme

We're closely related to gorillas.
In many ways, they're just like you, you see
But unlike you, they're rare
And the reason you should care?
It's because ...
They're members of your family!

The gorillas were a cuddly bunch.
The mothers hugged their babies, the sisters
groomed each other, and they touched
noses to greet each other. The guide told
us that in some cultures, people make
the same gesture.

I often
touch noses
with Cyril.

Scruffy's Gorilla Dictionary

Sound and posture	Meaning
Open mouth, no teeth showing	We're friends.
Humming, singing, lower lip hanging	I've found a good banana.
Throwing sticks, chest beating, roaring	I'm the boss!
Belching, grooming	We enjoyed those bananas.
Clapping, hooting	Look out, danger!

By now, the park was nearly closing, and it was time to go. I'd learnt how to talk like a tiger, a bee, an octopus, an elephant and a gorilla. But there's only one animal who *truly* understands me.

Is it a penguin? A rhino? A hippo?

No, it's my dog, Scruffy!

Talk to the hand

Can gorillas understand words? Yes! In 1971, a gorilla called Koko learnt over 2,000 words using American Sign Language. She made up her own sentences and even told jokes.

gorilla

sorry

Koko

love

ask

hungry

eat

drink

tickle

good

67

Glossary

abdomen the tail end of insects or tummy part of mammals

ceremony a way of celebrating

epilepsy a brain condition that can cause fits

freshwater water that is not salty – freshwater fish live in rivers and lakes

gestures body movements which express thoughts

marine related to the sea – marine fish live in the sea

pollen fine yellow powder made by flowers

tropical a hot, rainy place – tropical fish live in the water in and around hot countries

unique the only one of its kind

variety a mixture

Index

About the author

How did you get into writing?

I've been writing stories since I was five years old and never stopped. I had my first book published when I was 21. As a child, I wrote the books on plain paper in pencil then stitched the pages together. I still have those little books half a century later! Sometimes, my big sister illustrated

Jeanne Willis

them because she was much better at drawing than me – at least that's what she told me!

What do you hope readers will get out of the book?

I hope they will learn that animals are not 'dumb creatures' at all and that they all have their own unique ways of communicating.

Is there anything in this book that relates to your own experiences?

I'm fascinated by all creatures, great and small. And I've always wanted to 'talk to the animals' like Dr Doolittle, a character in the famous books written by Hugh Lofting.

What is it like for you to write?

It's like going into a trance, in a time warp. Hours flash by without me noticing. It's hard to picture not writing.

What is a book you remember loving reading when you were young?

There are so many, but one I loved was *Stig of the Dump*.

What's your best example of an amazing way that animals communicate?

Animals that leave messages in their wee always get my vote!

Do you have any pets? What have you learnt about the ways they communicate?

I've had so many pets including dogs, cats, rabbits, ferrets, toads, frogs, newts, fish, snakes, rats and insect species. I breed exotic beetles, keep mantids and Giant African snails and I foster hedgehogs. Did you know rats vibrate and grind their teeth when they're happy?

If you could speak the language of one animal, which one would you choose?

I'd like to speak to a caterpillar and ask what it wanted to be when it grew up – what if it didn't want to be a moth or a butterfly and it said, "a tiger!"?

About the illustrator

What made you want to be an illustrator?

When I was little I read a lot of picture books and those pictures made me dream. When I grew up I wanted to be able to do the same thing through my drawings. I like knowing that now my books make other people dream and at the same time teach them things.

Isabella Grott

What did you like best about illustrating this book?

I really enjoyed drawing different animals and also the different poses of Scruffy, the dog. It was a lot of fun!

Is there anything in this book that relates to your own experiences?

This book made me remember one of the best days I experienced when I was a child! It was when I went with my Dad to the zoo near my town for the first time. I still remember the happiness of seeing all those animals. It was a great feeling to relive it all through this book.

How do you bring a character to life?

You have to study, take photo references (very often I take photos of myself playing the character) and draw until you are convinced. Inventing the characters is my best part.

How do you approach drawing animals? Do you use pictures, or observe animals in real life, or use your imagination (or all three)?

To draw the animals I do an image search and find lots of pictures of the animal in different poses. Then I add some of my imagination and draw the animal until I am satisfied!

Do you prefer drawing animals or drawing people? Why?

I prefer drawing animals and plants, they have been my great passion since childhood and I never get bored! Whenever I draw animals I always learn new things.

Do you have any pets? Is it easy to communicate with them?

I grew up in the country and always had animals – dogs, cats and rabbits. Now I live in the city with my cat. At first I didn't know cats well so I didn't really know how to communicate with her. Now, it's easy for me to understand what she wants to tell me. I watch her movements (of her tail, ears) and understand what she wants to say.

Book chat

What was the most interesting thing you learnt from reading the book?

If you could give the author one piece of advice to improve the book, what would it be?

If you had to give the book a new title, what would you choose?

Which part of the book surprised you most? Why?

Do you have a pet? Can you understand what it is trying to tell you?

Which animal in the book did you think communicated in the strangest way?

If you could ask the author one question, what would it be?

Did this book remind you of anything you have experienced in real life?

Book challenge:

Think of another animal you like. Do some research to find out how that animal communicates.

Collins
BIG CAT

Published by Collins
An imprint of HarperCollins*Publishers*

The News Building
1 London Bridge Street
London SE1 9GF
UK

Macken House
39/40 Mayor Street Upper
Dublin 1
D01 C9W8
Ireland

10 9 8 7 6 5 4

ISBN 978-0-00-862457-6

British Library Cataloguing-in-Publication Data
A catalogue record for this publication is available
from the British Library.

Download the teaching notes and
word cards to accompany this book at:
http://littlewandle.org.uk/signupfluency/

Get the latest Collins Big Cat news at
collins.co.uk/collinsbigcat

Author: Jeanne Willis
Illustrator: Isabella Grott (Astound Illustration
    Agency)
Publisher: Lizzie Catford
Product manager: Caroline Green
Series editor: Charlotte Raby
Development editor: Catherine Baker
Commissioning editor: Suzannah Ditchburn
Project manager: Emily Hooton
Content editor: Daniela Mora Chavarría
Copyeditor: Sally Byford
Phonics reviewer: Rachel Russ
Proofreader: Gaynor Spry
Cover designer: Sarah Finan
Typesetter: 2Hoots Publishing Services Ltd
Production controller: Katharine Willard

Collins would like to thank the teachers and
children at the following schools who took part in
the trialling of Big Cat for Little Wandle Fluency:
Burley And Woodhead Church of England Primary
School; Chesterton Primary School; Lady Margaret
Primary School; Little Sutton Primary School;
Parsloes Primary School.

Printed and bound in the UK by Page Bros Group Ltd

Acknowledgements
The publishers gratefully acknowledge the permission
granted to reproduce the copyright material in this
book. Every effort has been made to trace copyright
holders and to obtain their permission for the use of
copyright material. The publishers will gladly receive
any information enabling them to rectify any error or
omission at the first opportunity.

p34t Matthew Egginton/Shutterstock, p34c Nature
Picture Library/Alamy Stock Photo, p34b Sushaaa/
Shutterstock, p35t Marek Mierzejewski/Shutterstock,
p35tc Gary K Smith/Alamy Stock Photo, p35bc Frank
Hecker/Alamy Stock Photo, p35b ViewFinder/Alamy
Stock Photo, p46t World History Archive/Alamy Stock
Photo, p46b grafxart/Shutterstock, p47t BIOSPHOTO/
Alamy Stock Photo, p47b Helmut Corneli/Alamy
Stock Photo.